The Life and Times of Lilly the Lash®

Ocean Commotion
Written By Julie Woik

To Booker -
Please Help me Teach the World About
Honesty. Let's Show Everyone How Good
It Feels To Set Things Straight!!!!
Be A Great Leader! February
Yahooooo 2018

Snow in Sarasota Publishing, Inc.
Osprey, FL 34229
Library of Congress Cataloging in Publication Data
Woik Julie
Ocean Commotion
(Book #3 in The Life and Times of Lilly the Lash® series)

p. cm.
ISBN – 978-0-9824611-9-8
1. Fiction, Juvenile 2. Psychology, self-esteem 3. Multi-cultural

First Edition
10 9 8 7 6 5 4 3 2 1

Design: Elsa Kauffman
Illustration: Marc Tobin

Printed by Arcade Lithographing, Sarasota, Florida
in the United States of America

ABOUT THIS BOOK

The Life and Times of Lilly the Lash® is a series of fascinating children's books, in which an **EYELASH** teaches life lessons and the importance of strong self-esteem.

Adventurous, yet meaningful storylines told in rhythm and rhyme, accompanied by spectacular cinematic-like illustrations; provide the tomboyish main character with a marvelous opportunity to teach children valuable lessons, while entertaining at every turn.

These whimsical tales for boys and girls age 0 – 10 (to 110!), will break their world of imagination wide open, and transcend their hearts and souls beyond their wildest dreams.

In book three of the series, *Ocean Commotion*, Lilly the Lash finds herself in the town of Rockin' Reef, where the mysterious disappearance of store items leaves an entire community in distress, and a young octopus pursuing the merits of **HONESTY.** Lilly, only ever seen by the reader, sends in a cool and caring shrimp to help the octopus realize the effects of her actions; prompting her to stand tall, accept responsibility, and set things straight!

LEARNING ACTIVITIES

Be sure to check out Lilly's website **www.lillythelash.com** to find the array of **FREE** Lesson Plans, Crafting Activities, and Games created for various age ranges and multiple learning levels. These amazing activities are designed for the educational community in a classroom setting, as well as the family structure in a home environment.

Your Actions Affect
EVERYONE

DEDICATION

To my husband Finn
The warmth of your affections
have melted me to a sea of liquid gold.
Thank you for making me feel so precious!

Your Adoring Wife

OCEAN COMMOTION

Book #3 in the Series
The Life and Times of Lilly the Lash®

While soaring the skies, Lilly hoped she would find,
The most beautiful place to relax and unwind.
As she peered through the clouds, Lilly's wish had come true,
"A paradise," she said, "with a marvelous view."

A miscalculation to land on the ledge,
Left Lilly one handed just over the edge.

"I may need more practice on landing in flight,
'Cause I think I'd have fallen, if my grip wasn't tight!"

From the Cà d'Zan tower overlooking the bay,
Came a prism of light slowly drifting her way.
The rippling waves washed a bottle ashore,

With a message that read,

"WE'VE GOT TROUBLE GALORE!"

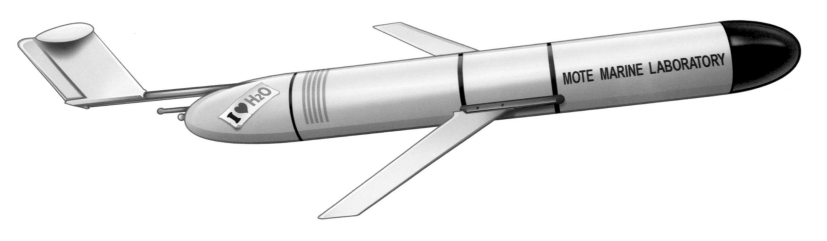

Devising a plan for the best way to cruise,
Lilly spotted a rocket the scientists used.
It stored information that served as their guide,
But could quickly transform to a supersonic ride.

Now before diving deeper, I'd like to make clear,
How Ms. Lilly's adventures have gotten us here.
It all had begun with a wink and a smile,
When this eyelash appeared on my face as a child.

At first I'll admit, she was quite a surprise,
But I'd soon come to realize that Lilly was wise.

There was something about how she'd help you to see,
That the future was now, and that YOU held the key.

She often viewed life through a magnifying glass,
Inspecting each moment before it would pass.

"You'll find," Lilly whispered, "if you look really close,
    Our values and morals are what matters the most."

mor • al (môr´ əl, mor´ -), *adj* . 1. exhibiti
goodness or correctness in character an
behavior. 2. pertaining to the standard
what is right or good. – *n.* 3. the lesso
principle taught by a fable.

more (mōr, môr), *adj* . 1. a greater
degree, amount, or measure. 2. f
in addition to. 3. something of g
importance.

orn • ing (môr´ning), *n.* 1.
day; the dawn. 2. the
the day.

mo ō´shən),
process ving or
tion. 2. power of

While the years spent together
had strengthened our bond,
I could see Lilly's gift
stretching far and beyond.
I knew then and there
it was best to let go,
Of the one whom I loved,
and watched over my soul.

age 8

age 5½

age 3

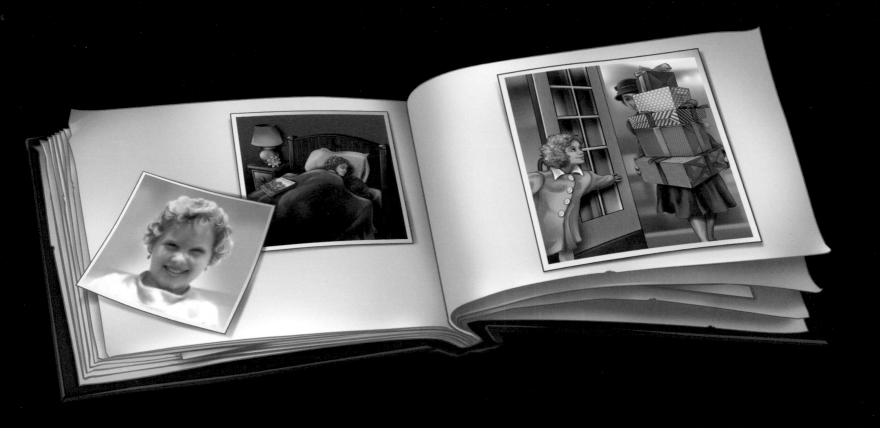

As the quiet of darkness brought close to the day,
Lilly pondered her thoughts before slipping away.

She stepped from my cheek
and glanced fondly below,
Then took to the sky
with her child-like glow.

It's time we head back to that watery road,
Where Ms. Lilly sits waiting to enter the code.
With the missile on course and the light flashing green,
She braced for the ride, shouting "Thanks Mote Marine!"

Lilly's main target was somewhere outside,
    The town *Rockin' Reef*, where the problem resides.
"There it is!" Lilly cried as she lowered the flap,
    "The precise destination marked X on the map."

The hub of the action was always at Peg's.
A great place for games or just resting your legs.

You could share with your neighbor,
your hopes and your dreams,

While you watched Puffer Peg
whip up candies and creams.

But something upsetting was causing a stir,
And folks were now feeling a tad insecure.
With items gone missing and no one to blame,
The mood in the village was one in the same.

While settling into a shell on the sand,
Lilly caught sight of the crisis at hand.

She saw a young octopus stretch out her arm,
To snatch a gold necklace and sand dollar charm.

Echo raced off to her home by the pier,
Filled with excitement, she gazed in the mirror.
"Wowwww, look at this," Echo squealed with delight,
"It matches the earrings I took from Orange Kite."

There were no second thoughts to what Echo had done,
She was thrilled with these things she had taken in fun.
She was thinking of only herself in this case,
Unaware that her conduct, could bring her disgrace.

Down at the plaza where everyone shops,
    A Trunk Full of Trinkets had phoned in the cops.
The landlord, Ms. Casey, asked Officer Snout,
        "Just how can we stop all this messing about?"

"A community meeting is what I'd suggest,
To voice your concerns of this unwanted guest.
An exchange of ideas would also relieve,
Your building frustration from being deceived."

TOWN MEETING
Saturday Morning
at 9:00AM

Hairy the barber
from Old Clipper Ship,

Called out
to the policeman,

"Hey, thanks for the tip!"

And by that afternoon
they had posted a sign,

To gather
on Saturday morning
at nine.

But before the week's end, Echo strolled into town,
To grab a new lipstick to go with her gown.

And although she had almost been caught by the Queen,
She had once again managed to get away clean.

At the edge of the reef, Lilly stood near the fence,
Untangling the ongoing string of events.
She planned to help Echo to see her mistake,
"If it's not yours to have, then it's not yours to take."

And with that, Echo answered a knock at the door.
It was Jackson, her friend from the video store.

He had brought a large pizza and gummy worms too.
An incredible combo too good to be true!

"You goin'," Jack inquired, "to the Rockin' Reef Square?"
"Why would I?" Echo asked, as she pulled up a chair.
"Well tomorrow they're going to discuss an alarm,
    To stop the intruder from causing more harm."

"What's the big deal?" Echo wondered out loud,
"I can hardly believe this would draw up a crowd.
There's so many things in a store they can sell,
That when something is gone, I'm surprised they can tell."

SALE!

NEW

BUBBLES   BUBBLES

20% OFF

Well, Jack could relate, as it happened to him.
His watch had been stolen right out of the gym.
"I'll never forget how I suffered that day,
I was angry and sad and felt very betrayed."

About to head out, Jackson tried to explain,
How the shops lose their money and feel the same pain.
"But for me," Jack revealed, "it was not in the cost.
What it meant to my heart, would forever be lost."

The cue for Ms. Lilly
to gear up and fly,
Had come with a wave
and a friendly good-bye.
As Echo watched Jack
disappear down the street,
She realized that **SHE**
was the cause of deceit.

Spiraling up from between the two decks,
Lilly tossed handfuls of shimmering flecks.
Trickling down onto Echo with grace,
A magical lash soon appeared on her face.

A clear understanding had come into light.
And Echo could see what she'd done wasn't right.
The first break of day would allow her the chance,
To address her behavior and take a new stance.

Echo arrived to find Peg in a state.
So she shot to the front, to set everything straight.
"The commotion", she declared to the public at large,
"I have brought on myself, and am guilty as charged."

"I haven't been honest," she cried in despair,
  "And I've caused others harm, when I wasn't aware.
I'll return all the merchandise back to the stores,
  And promise the owners to do extra chores."

Everyone quietly stared up at the stage.
The feeling among them no longer was rage.
With Echo's confession, the folks were quite pleased.
She had made her amends, bringing calm to the seas.

The silence broke free once the music began,
And the town filled with laughter according to plan.

For Ms. Lilly the Lash,
this whole case was now closed,
As for what lies ahead,
well...nobody knows.

The End

. . . are you sure?

FUN FACTS

 The Cà d'Zan (Cà dă zăn), meaning "House of John", is located on the bay in beautiful Sarasota, Florida. Built in the 1920's, this breathtaking structure was the home to John and Mable Ringling, of the Ringling Brothers family circus.

 The Slocum Glider, used by the Mote Marine Laboratory, is an amazing tool that collects data from our ocean waterways. These sleek rocket-shaped machines gather important scientific information, and transmit the findings back to base through a satellite system. What a clever devise, aye?!

 Reefs are frequently referred to as the "Rainforests of the Sea." These spectacular coral dwellings provide shelter for 25% of all marine life, and supply tasty, nutritious meals for 30-40 million human beings every year.

 Puffer fish are remarkable creatures. Their unusual design allows them to convert to a rigid, almost perfectly-shaped sphere, by inflating their body to 3 times its size, leaving potential attackers confused and frightened. Boo!

 An octopus has 2 eyes, 8 legs, and 3 hearts. They're highly intelligent and have an excellent sense of touch. Swimming and crawling are common forms of travel, however, jet propulsion is utilized when the need is speed!!

 Jellyfish have existed for over 650 million years. Whoa...that's longer than the dinosaurs! Coming in a variety of sizes, and an array of vibrant colors, these graceful organisms are often viewed as extraordinary works of art.

 Did you know that manatees are closely related to the elephant? An adult can average about 10 ft. in length and weigh between 800 and 1,200 lbs. They can swim up to 20 mph, but tend to keep a pace of about 3-5 mph.

 Queen Triggerfish are simply magnificent. They'll dazzle you with their distinctive glow-like markings, and their unique ability to adjust their shade from light to dark, depending on their mood. An incredible sight to behold.

 Shrimp have this awesome ability to swim both forward and backward. With a high tolerance for toxins, they often eat what others pass by. Unfortunately for them, they're a great food source for larger animals!

Lilly's kickin' it Back
(Back to the country that is!)

The Life and Times of Lilly the Lash®
The Kacklin' Kitchen

A sweet summer's morning was just the right thing,
To supply the young birds with a song they could sing.
From a long crooked branch that reached out like a hand,
They had gathered together to strike up the band.

An audience grew, joining in on the fun,
Playing all of the instruments under the sun.
A cobblestone chimney, a few houses down,
Had offered Ms. Lilly the best seat in town.

About to take off, Lilly happened to see,
Through a wide open window, the place she should be.
The eggs on the table were throwing a fit,
While the cheese and the butter were threatening to split!

(Watch for Book #4 in this Series)

Follow Lilly on her next adventure to
Cobblestone Cove
Where a young carton of milk learns the important
Life Lesson of
RESPECT

SPECIAL THANKS

To Marc - Lilly's Incredible Illustrator
Every image on every page is
ABSOLUTE MAGIC!
I cherish the fact that I get to work with someone
whose extraordinary talent and creativity are simply unmatched.
(And you're really quite funny you know!!)
Thank you for loving Lilly and taking her to new dimensions.

To Elsa - My Design Guru
What an incredible journey life is.
I'm so glad I have you to walk with, down the many roads that lie ahead.
Your kindnesses envelop me when I need them most.
Thank you for being a shining star in my universe!

To Lisa Heim - (The Idea-nator)
Every time I'm in need of pulling together
the intricate details that surround some
super fantastic project or activity I've decided to create…
you're able to brainstorm the idea to make it the best it can be.
I hope you know how much you mean to me.

To My Fabulous Parents
You two are such an inspiration!
Each and every day I strive to carry out the important
character building lessons you have so graciously taught me.
Living in such times of uncertainty, I'm comforted by the fact that
your unconditional love and encouragement will always be there
to guide and point me in whatever direction I may need to go.
I love you more than you could ever possibly know.

Very Special Thanks
To the ever so lovely Michael and Kitty
for stepping into our world at a time when we most needed you.
Your belief in Lilly and everything she stands for,
has completely overwhelmed us.

Making Our World

A Better Place

A percentage of the profit from
this book will go to the:

**cf® Cystic
Fibrosis
Foundation**

Specifying: Research

For the tomorrows of
two fantastic young ladies
Alexandria and Aundrianna Twigg
and their incredible mother Natalie...my hero.

As warriors do, they live their lives
with the courage and grace we all should aspire to!

Forever in my heart. Love, Julie